Thank God for the Shelter

Memoirs of a Homeless Healer

(2nd Edition)

Thank God for the Shelter:

Memoirs of a Homeless Healer

(2nd Edition)

ISBN 978-1540334589

Dedication

This book is dedicated to healing artists, past and present, who hold sacred spaces for creative genius to transmute pain and suffering into joy and peace.

Body workers, energy healers, naturopaths, spiritual healers, ministers, counselors, coaches, care-takers, teachers, artists: You are God's gift to the world.

Remember self-care is the manifestation of self-love. Whenever you find yourself feeling out of sync or discombobulated; reflect on your daily self-care activities or the lack thereof. The well-being of the world is in your hands.

Acknowledgments

Since publishing my first book in 2008, I've met some of the most amazingly gifted light workers. They have challenged me to think critically, expand my cosciousness, and see a world filled with ever expanding good. I especially want to acknowledge the following ministers and teachers for being examples of *God manifested:* Honorable Akhenaten S'L'M-Bey, Delano Willis, Kimle Nailer, Rev. Kania Kennedy, Rev. Andre Kennebrew, Dr. Zenobia Day, Latron Price, Rev. Claude La Vertu, Devita Mosley and Abdullah Bey.

There is no greater experience than being in the presence of God. Through these individuals' expression of Love, I have experienced heaven on earth and I am inspired to travel the world teaching love and peace through Conscious Affirmative Living as it has been demonstrated to me. Because of these individuals, I know that God is not an invisible force that lives in the clouds, and that miracles are not unique to the days and times of Jesus Christ.

Thank God for my divine dream team who always appears right on time. Thank you, Autwan Fuller; photographic artist, Demetrius Smith III; multimedia artist, and Claude La Vertu; editor – you have made the 2nd Edition of *Thank God for the Shelter* a blueprint for overcoming adversity while connecting to the power within.

Shelter:

Protection from danger or bad weather

Place of refuge

Sanctuary

Haven

Security

Covering

Home

Foreword

Integrity. No other word better defines the unification of commitment, discipline, devotion and *"love in action"* as does the word integrity. And, no other human being I have ever met better embodies the word integrity than does Versandra Kennebrew.

Whether I'm requested to speak in defense of a great cause, or write a letter of recommendation for a business colleague, or write a foreword for a book, I ask myself whether or not the individual for whom I am writing is somebody whose principles are worth defending to the point of actually laying down my life. I take very seriously the privilege of defending and promoting others–a privilege for which so many people in so many countries willingly die–and as such, in regards to the fruits of their labor, something must absolutely be worth my word; because my word is worth my life. This exceptional little book holds such merit.

Versandra and her book are one and the same. They are honest, loving, joyous and profoundly intelligent. They nourish, they guide, they teach, they give...they understand. I've had the blessed opportunity to participate in the editing and publishing process of countless books over several years, but there's something so pure and precious about this particular book and about its magnificent author that words simply don't do justice to any form of accolade. This is not a book that one reads, but which one must "live" in order to truly experience.

Versandra's love for humanity and her drive to exhaust her every resource–every single day–in order to do her part to make the world a better place, has inspired, and continues to inspire, countless thousands of individuals worldwide to do the same. I am one of those people. Versandra changed my life the day I met her, and I continue to grow and evolve as a result of having this beautiful, blessed soul in my life. A soul by which to be held accountable, by which to be inspired, by which to measure true greatness among so many already great individuals, and by which to be loved.

I first met Versandra at a weekend-long *health and healing* conference in Montreal, Quebec (Canada) where we'd both been invited to speak on the topic of holistic healing. Of the many illustrious speakers and coaches from diverse fields of healing who were presenting that weekend, it was undeniably Versandra who stole the show. With her ability to engage the entire audience, and her loving approach to getting people to "commit" to themselves and their lives and their dreams and goals, she came away the fan favorite, bar none! Perhaps what stood out the most about Versandra was that she was already a star in her own right.

Beyond her innate "star quality", what makes Versandra a true expert in her field as well as a profoundly effective personal development coach, teacher and speaker, is her personal hands-on life experience. In this day and age of recycled data coming from many would-be, wanna-be experts, Versandra is one of the precious few who knows what they're talking about and who knows what works; because she's *been there* and has the bumps, bruises, scrapes, aches and pains to prove it; along with a whole lot of sage wisdom and a magnificent story with which to inspire others.

Beyond the inspiring story of overcoming adversity, lessons on the manifesting process, and powerful practical exercises, *"Thank God For The Shelter"* demystifies what most people have come to understand about what it means to be homeless; helping people understand that it's okay to have been there, or to be there, or to go there if necessary for there is *healing* there.

This book is a labor of love by someone whose every word and every motive is rooted in pure love. It is that same love that saw her through the most challenging times of her life so that she could bring her message to the entire world. Thank you Versandra; for your message, for your love, and for your integrity.

~Claude La Vertu

Introduction

"I searched for God and found only myself. I search for myself and found only God." ~Rumi

It has been a pleasure sharing my story of triumph over adversity with nearly a million people all around the world. As a homeless advocate speaking at conferences and universities, my story is about how a professional becomes homeless and learns to survive and thrive again. As a minister, empowering and inspiring shelter guests and people in transition – on the bus, on the streets and on countless radio, news and television programs – my story and the activities in this book offer a roadmap to healing and transformation.

When I was homeless, I felt destitute, hopeless and worthless. I thought people who looked wealthy had no clue what I was going through. Later I learned that there was abundant wealth and love surrounding me. So much so, absolute strangers came to my aide physically, spiritually and financially, as I became clear about what I wanted for my own life.

With much humility, I will share with you how I made it through the darkest days of my life. You will have the opportunity to practice exercises that gave me insight and strength to overcome the depression and addictions that led me to the shelter and empowered me to attain a level of success I never thought possible. I have also provided you with some of my favorite words of inspiration that lifted me when I was down. In addition, you will find areas to help you create your own affirmations which are *definitive prayers.*

In this memoir, I hope to encourage you to never give up. Whether you live in the shelter of a soon-to-be foreclosed home, your place of business, an extended stay hotel, or a car parked in a cemetery that you've been hiding from the repo-man, I want to inspire you to unimaginable heights. I want to introduce you to your divine self like you've never known before.

As you read this powerful story and begin to write, speak and visualize the life you truly desire, be open and prepared for a new perspective on living an abundant life. In addition to the exercises and affirmations in this book, you may find solace in journaling or writing down your thoughts in the space provided. So grab a pen or pencil and insert your name below to personalize this statement. Keep your pen or pencil close by so you can complete the exercises included in this interactive book.

Today, I _____

promise to utilize my time in the shelter to gain strength and knowledge, and to be supported. I accept this temporary reprieve as a period of reflection and personal and spiritual development.

I am committed to looking *within* for the answers I seek. I am eager to be whole again so that I can be a light for others experiencing life transitions.

Table of Contents

Find A Place of Refuge………………………………......1

Count Your Blessings……………………………17

Look In the Mirror…………………………………...35

Forgive Yourself and Others………………………48

Be Open to Opportunities……………………….......62

Watch Your Mouth……………………………….89

Believe You Can………………………………...105

Surround Yourself with Love and Beauty…………120

About the Author…………………………………141

Other Publications…………………………….....143

Chapter 1

Find A Place of Refuge

I remember that cold winter night like it was yesterday. I was in the relaxation studio, where I provided massages for the hotel guests. I looked over my thousand-dollar monthly invoice, and I wondered if the repo man was going to snatch my car while I was sleeping. How could I get to a client's home to provide a massage if I didn't have a car? If they repossessed my car, not only would I still have to pay the debt for a car I didn't have, I would also mess up my dad's credit because he had co-signed the car sales agreement for me.

I thought about how embarrassed I would be if I didn't pay the bill and they put me out of the hotel. For a brief moment, my mind even wandered to the day that I almost drove off a bridge to end the horrible feeling of anxiety boiling inside of me. So much was going through my head that night. I was desperate for relief.

I continued to look at my bills against the money I was bringing in, and it became as clear as day: I was broke. I had no money and no home. I had been fooling myself for a long time, but reality was finally kicking in. I was depressed and unable to function optimally because I was stressed to the max in every way possible. I was angry and there was no end in sight.

We do not see with our eyes, you know. The images before us are merely illusions our brain conjures up. Depending on our state of mind, backgrounds, beliefs and feelings; what we think

2

we see may not be real. Our very complex computers called *brains* just spit out images based on our skewed perceptions. But there is one thing indisputable: Numbers don't lie. In the red is *in the red*, no matter how you look at it.

For several hours I contemplated, ranted and raved in my head about my plight; overdrawn bank account, eviction, poor credit and so forth. In a brief moment of sanity, I read an email from a young lady named Kania whom I had never met before. She was telling me about a space for rent inside the Northwest Activities Center in Detroit. I had never even heard of that place. It didn't have a website, but she seemed to think it would be perfect for my business and me.

I could cut my business expenses, and then I could move into low-cost housing and turn my car in while I got myself back on track, I thought. For that moment, I could see a little spark of hope, and I wanted to keep it in view for as long as I could.

In the days to follow, I was desperate to do as much as I could before my depression kicked in again. I researched the city's northwest demographics, gathered my business paperwork, prepared a proposal for facility rental and looked for low-cost housing. My budget was about $250 per month. How in the world was I going to find decent, secure housing for that amount? Besides, my credit was jacked up and I was going to be without a car.

I could feel that I was quickly falling into depression again. My doctor had diagnosed me with premenstrual dysphoric disorder (PMDD). This condition is a severe form of PMS found primarily in women over 35. It is marked by depression, anxiety, mood swings and fatigue. About a week before menstruation I would begin to feel this uncontrollable rage building inside of me. So, I cried. I couldn't focus and I wanted to sleep for at least a week while the depression passed through its most severe stage, which coincidently ended as my body's cleansing began.

I had been fighting PMDD with prayer, meditation and relaxation therapies, but with all the stuff going on in my life, my willpower and faith were low. I had taken medication and received counseling before, but I was a holistic health professional and medication was not my preferred remedy. I had to do something drastic right away. My sanity was at stake.

In my retail career, one of my mentors taught me that when sales were below plan, you should cut those expenses that could be controlled to make sure you didn't have to close stores or lay off employees. Control the controllables. That would be my plan.

That night, while surfing the net, my search engine guided me to the Coalition on Temporary Shelter's (COTS) website. I located the phone number and called that night, leaving a message that I needed emergency shelter. My day had been long and tedious, so I decided to take a hot lavender bath to help me sleep. My tears were my prayers because I could not come up with the right words to say. I remembered other times when my groans had been heard by God and doors opened. I desperately needed that intercession again. I just wanted to sleep and be taken away from all the madness of this world.

A few days later, my call to the shelter was returned. I was told there wasn't any space at *Peggy's Place*, a facility for women and children within walking distance of my business. I was devastated and went to Peggy's Place in hopes of pleading my case. I tried to maintain my composure, but I could not hold back the tears. I was at my wit's end.

I could not handle any more disappointment or bad news. Something had to give. I thank God for the person who reviewed my case and stamped it "approved." I had already sold most of my possessions to get food to eat; everything I owned was in a few boxes in my hotel room. All I needed to do was pick them up and prepare to start over again. But first, I had to turn in my car.

It was December 2003. I walked up the front stairs into the lobby of the shelter, where a woman directed me to sign in. My body was shaking with fear. I had no idea what to expect. I had only seen shelters on television and in movies, and none of them looked like places I would want to live. She directed me up a flight of stairs and told me to turn right, and go to the end of the hallway. My room was the last door on the right. Room #205 would be my home for the next nine months.

Affirmations

Repeat the following affirmations out loud three times a day for the next seven days. See, feel and enjoy each experience as you say the affirmation.

In the space provided, use these affirmations as writing prompts. In the present tense, speak to your desired sense of security or enthusiasm for living.

My home is my safe haven.

I joyfully manage my money.

I love receiving and giving.

Exercise 1

Think about a time in your life when you were in need of shelter or a temporary place of refuge. Maybe it was after a breakup, a job loss or a medical emergency. Now reflect on factors that contributed to your need for others to provide you with security, a covering or sanctuary.

In the chart below, make a list of five factors in addition to the five already listed, and then check whether the factors on your list could have been controlled by you or not. It's important to be honest with yourself, because transparency is the first step to regaining control of your life. I have

Factors	I control	I don't control
Downsizing		X
Limited cash flow	X	
Emotional instability	X	
Divorce		X
Addiction	X	

listed five factors that contributed to my home-lessness.

It's easy to compare yourself to others or even beat yourself up for not being perfect. In this exercise, resist comparing your life challenge to anyone else's. For instance, I was addicted to *people-pleasing* because my self-esteem was low due to long term oppression. I was insecure and believed I did not deserve the absolute best of life. You and I have not had the same life experiences as you will learn in this story, so your response to life challenges will be different than mine.

When I completed this exercise, I felt like I was in control of my self-image and knowledge of who I really was as an offspring of the Creator of all things. I was also aware of resources to manage my emotions and add other streams of income.

Use the area provided to write about areas in which you lack control and whether it matters or not in your future success.

Journal

_____

_____

_____

_____

_____

_____

_____

_____

_____

_____

_____

_____

_____

_____

_____

_____

_____

_____

_____

_____

_____

_____

_____

_____

_____

_____

_____

_____

_____

_____

_____

_____

_____

_____

_____

_____

_____

_____

_____

_____

_____

_____

_____

_____

_____

_____

_____

_____

_____

_____

_____

_____

_____

_____

_____

_____

_____

_____

_____

_____

_____

Versandra Jewel Kennebrew

_____

_____

_____

_____

_____

_____

_____

_____

_____

_____

_____

_____

_____

_____

_____

Chapter 2

Count Your Blessings

Blessings are gifts that bestow favor, prosperity and welfare. You can be on the receiving end or the giving end and experience great joy. I had always been a giver and I had always felt fortunate. But on one snowy morning, I didn't feel very blessed.

The gloves and scarf a woman at the shelter gave me were just what I needed as I walked to work down McNichols in 10 degrees below zero weather. I knew I had to stay focused on the cars speeding by me, splashing filthy water as they passed, but tears blurred my vision. It was then these words came to me: *I have everything I need.*

My tears immediately turned to tears of joy. I had pep in my step as I walked and contemplated the words rolling around in my head and filling my spirit. I felt this message was divine. It resonated throughout my entire being.

Later that day, I shared my experience with a massage client. I knew I wasn't supposed to do that, but this client also was a friend. She reached for my hands and prayed for my strength, wisdom and peace of mind in the midst of my storm. "You are such an inspiration to me," she said, but on this day, I could not take credit. What happened earlier that day was simply a divine act. I was filled with peace and serenity.

That evening, as I prepared to walk home from my office, two of my neighbors at Northwest

Activities Center; Carl and Dewayne, were leaving and offered me a ride. I accepted, and made a wise crack about eating peanut butter and crackers for dinner.

At the shelter, about 16 families shared six bathrooms and two kitchens on each floor. I didn't go away to college, so I was in the dark about how community housing worked. You had to keep your food in your room if you didn't want it to disappear. If your food was frozen, it would more than likely remain that way until you cooked it. But fruit or snacks would be gone when you got back to the kitchen.

My friends didn't believe I lived in a shelter until I gave Dewayne directions. Soon thereafter, they took me to Kmart first and purchased groceries, dinnerware, cleaning supplies and an electric skillet. I told them my story as we shared a bottle of wine in the parking lot. I was pleased they didn't judge me, as I had judged others before becoming homeless myself.

My mind could not conceive I would ever live like this. I felt like a huge failure. Since I was 18, I had lived on my own, caring for myself. What was this life experience all about? What was the takeaway?

While living in Birmingham, AL, 15-years earlier, I took on the responsibility of being legal guardian to my younger brothers. My mother's mental illness caused her to be unable to care for us, and I desperately wanted to protect them from the things I thought no child should have to experience.

I got custody of my youngest brother after he fell from a third floor balcony. He wasn't quite two years old, and I was 23 with no children of my own. I couldn't let my brother Thaddeus be separated from our family and move from foster home to foster home. My grandmother had cared for my sister Sheila, my brother Isaac and me, and I wanted to follow her example. After she transtioned, I also accepted custody of Isaac so that my brothers could be together.

Now I was happy that Tad and Isaac were old enough to care for themselves, because I was 39 and homeless. I couldn't support them any longer. I couldn't protect them anymore.

In my mind, I reflected on being a child, living in the projects on Detroit's east side. The mice entertained us in our living room when we had company. They ate through steel wool used to block their points of entry, and they stole the cheese off the mouse traps. My grandma had us clean religiously. We had to scrub the floors and baseboards, remove everything from cabinets, wash them out and put roach powder down before lining the shelves with newspaper.

I promised myself I would never live in the projects or anyplace where roaches or mice also resided. I had not seen any rodents in my temporary home, but I felt I had broken my promise to myself. I felt like a huge failure.

Just a few years ago, I lived in a two-bedroom townhome with a loft, full basement and fireplace in Southfield, MI. I hosted pamper parties where ten to twenty women gathered in my home to enjoy footbaths, massages, facials, book signings and music. No pamper parties were going on in the shelter. Everyone there seemed to have a dark cloud over them. Sadness and despair was in the air.

Was it my three divorces that had brought me to this place? Was it the closing of Edison Brother Stores January 2000, just as I accepted my calling as a healer and enrolled in school to become a massage therapist? Perhaps it was the grief associ-

22

ated with my two miscarriages? I heard a lot of other people blame their situations on the aftermath of September 11, 2001. Maybe that was it?

I was broken and homeless. I couldn't find a decent job. Interviewers said I was overqualified. "Overqualified to eat!?" I asked. "If a man don't work, a man don't eat," I'd sarcastically retort when I saw homeless people before. But now I was that homeless person. I was willing to work, and had skills to offer any company that would hire me.

In the shelter, once inhabited by nuns, my mind wandered back to the morning I received the divine revelation: *I have everything I need.* I meditated on those words and wrote down every blessing I received that day.

By the time I went to bed that night, I resolved everyone would receive the gift of massage for Christmas that year. Even strangers would be invited to receive free massages. I wanted to give, and I was testing myself to see if I really had everything I needed.

I tried to sleep, but the stress I had been under for so long kept my mind wandering. Thoughts of my business haunted me. I had big dreams. I wanted to be a massage therapist, but I also wanted to do something that would make Detroit a healthier place to live. The energy here was nothing like the energy in Maryland. It seemed like everyone around me was complaining and depressed.

I was struggling, trying to transition from being a service provider to the executive director of an association of complementary and alternative medicine (CAM) professionals, because I knew that people needed to be educated about holistic therapies before they would embrace them. I wanted to gather all of the struggling CAM professionals together to educate the masses. That was my goal. I figured that once people were educated, they would line up to learn more about a natural approach to wellness. I was wrong.

The CAM professionals in Detroit did not want to come together, and the community I served could not have cared less about embracing a holistic lifestyle. I was beginning to feel like the others, and that wasn't an option. I had to shake this negativity.

"Give and you shall receive, good measure, pressed down, shaken together and running over." That's what I'd been taught. "Why wasn't I receiving?" "What was I doing wrong?" I asked myself over and over. One of my spiritual leaders said to me, "Be not weary in well doing, for in due season you will reap if you faint not." And yet, I was still getting the message I have everything I needed. How was this possible? I had to open my eyes.

Dear reader, if you have a highlighter, use it here: *You cannot see if your eyes are closed.* This simply means when you are in a crisis, you get tunnel vision. You are focused on the problem so deeply you are sometimes blinded to the solution. Your eyes are closed to infinite possibilities.

I must say, however, if this is you, you are not alone. Many of us were raised by parents who lived in survival mode all their lives. "We are all just surviving," one of my cousins often said. She said we can't take on other people's problems; they have to learn to survive for themselves.

I have chosen not to embrace survival mode and struggling just to stay alive with limited resources and growth potential. In fact, when I see it rear its ugly head, I shout, "I thrive – not survive!" Say it with me now: "I thrive – not survive!"

The difference between surviving and thriving is like owning a massage business or owning a massage franchise. One business model is home-based earning just enough to pay the bills. The other is leveraged by a team of well trained experts. The first operates in survival mode, with minimal expenses or requirements. The second operates so its entire team can thrive, serving a multitude with multiple revenue streams.

Seventeen years of caring for two children who weren't mine, three divorces, corporate downsizing, the aftermath of the September 11 terrorist attacks and going out of business, were all crisis situations. I survived these tests to learn how to thrive. "Be still and know that I am God," was my greatest lesson. It took me several years, but I got it. I needed to go back to school and reinforce my unstable foundation.

I'm convinced it took me so long to learn the lesson because I had been forced to lead since I was young. I was the oldest sister, a surrogate mother, young retail manager, entrepreneur and holistic health educator. I had little higher education, so I educated myself by reading business books and attending weekend workshops. I was running around in circles chasing a dream.

My body was telling me something was wrong. Bouts with depression and anxiety were signs of exhaustion and malnutrition. It was clear; rest was a good thing, not a sign of failure. The shelter was a blessing in disguise. It would protect me and allow me to heal. The shelter was my place to rest while I regrouped.

Affirmations

Repeat the following affirmations out loud three times a day for the next few days. See, feel and enjoy each experience as you say each affirmation.

Each person I meet is blessed with a smile or kind word.

I am as God created me.

Happiness is recognizing miracles are everywhere.

I am a life-long learner.

I am self-care conscious.

Exercise 2

In the space provided, contemplate, then write about five blessings you have *received* in the past 24 hours. Also write about five ways you have been a blessing to others. If you can't remember ten blessings, envision blessings you would like and write about them.

Versandra Kennebrew

Journal

_____

_____

_____

_____

_____

_____

_____

_____

_____

_____

_____

_____

_____

_____

Versandra Kennebrew

_____

_____

_____

_____

_____

_____

_____

_____

_____

_____

_____

_____

_____

_____

Thank God for The Shelter: Memoirs of a Homeless Healer

_____

_____

_____

_____

_____

_____

_____

_____

_____

_____

_____

_____

_____

_____

_____

_____

Versandra Kennebrew

_____

_____

_____

_____

_____

_____

_____

_____

_____

_____

_____

_____

_____

_____

_____

Chapter Three

Look In the Mirror

I woke up one morning and looked at the bare white walls around my room, and I reflected on the three years before moving into the shelter. I had moved back to Michigan from Maryland to care for my father who had been diagnosed with prostate cancer. My father had tried many times to get me to move back home because he was concerned about me raising my two brothers with no family around. He suggested that I move in with him, take a part-time job and go back to school. This time, I agreed.

Before the move, I was virtually debt- free and made more than $50,000 annually as a retail market manager. Each day I travelled around "The Beltway" in my brand new company car, training and developing up to 60 managers in 22 stores. But three years of soul-searching led me to begin a more fulfilling career as a massage therapist. I was ready to carry out my life's purpose.

My family and friends could not understand why I wasn't content with having a "good job." I knew I had more to offer to the world. I also knew my spiritual journey led me to my decision. My father's cancer diagnosis brought me to Michigan to pursue my new career as a massage therapist, and I was also able to help him during his recovery.

As I continued to reflect on how I got to this place, I thought about the day when I learned the company I worked for would close its doors. Nine years of service would end on January 1, 2000, less than a year after relocating. I never did receive my severance package. Bummer!

My options were to go back to Maryland to take a comparable position in retail, or continue my massage education and begin an unknown journey of healing.

I did not want to look back five years later with regret. Besides, I thought my life experiences to this point had prepared me to handle any challenge. I chose the unknown journey. It would take me on a roller coaster ride, testing my faith and revealing my fears. I thought my new profession was to heal others, but I discovered that I too needed to be healed.

The reflection in the mirror was of a confused woman who had been fighting for her life for too long. *"I searched for God and found only myself. I searched for myself and found only God."* I remembered this quote from somewhere, and it seemed to give me comfort. As long as I could remember, I had been seeking truth, seeking God.

I believe my move to Detroit was simply another phase of my purging. There was more that I had to give up. There were attitudes, prejudices and habits that I had to let go of. My father was healed of cancer, but there were miracles, more acts of God on the way.

The shelter had to teach me that God was in everything and everybody, including the man searching for food in a garbage can. I also had to learn that everything happened in divine order. I was not in control of everything. The *God in me* was in control.

It was time for me to step out of the fear that was holding me back from my purpose, and step into my divine greatness. I had to release fear. I had to "let go and let God." The growing pains would hurt, but it had to be done.

Before I moved forward, I had to take an honest look at how my life choices had contributed to my downfall. The picture had to be clear so that I would not make the same mistakes. I couldn't take procrastination or laziness with me. I had to find balance, and I had to be healed of all I had gone through in my life.

I was not going to be crazy like my mother. I was not going to cut people with razors and end up in jail or a psychiatric hospital. I was not going to abandon my children. I was not going to be gang-raped as retaliation for crimes I had committed. I was not going to be addicted to drugs or alcohol. I was not going to be weak...

I was not going to be my mom!

Affirmations

Repeat the following affirmations out loud three times a day for the next few days. See, feel and enjoy each experience as you say the affirmation. In the space provided, write three affirmations in the present tense that reflect how you feel as an offspring of the Most High.

My mind, body and spirit work in symphony.

My life is filled with love, joy and prosperity.

I am attracting wealth in every aspect of my life.

Exercise 3

On the circle of life below, place a dot on the line to rate where you feel you are in your life today. The center of the circle is equivalent to 0 and the outer bold line is 10.

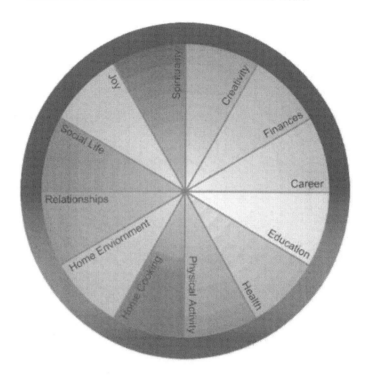

Now, connect your dots and imagine what you have created is the wheel on a car. How far down the road would it get? What three areas will you commit to enhancing your knowledge about and experience in to make your life more balanced and fulfilled?

When I was homeless, I did monitor my finances. It was unfortunate that I only checked to see how broke I was. I had a lack mentality. I should have kept track of my finances daily, to be inspired by its growth. Whether it was another ten dollars or additional thousand dollars, it was the manifestation of the value I brought to the world.

When we focus our attention and intention on being happy, productive and rich, we manifest that. Think about some of the things that make you happy, make you most productive and make you feel rich. Meditate on these things night and day.

In the space provided, write about what you see when you look in the mirror. How does it make you feel?

Journal

_____

_____

_____

_____

_____

_____

_____

_____

_____

_____

_____

_____

_____

_____

_____

_____

_____

_____

_____

_____

_____

_____

_____

_____

_____

_____

_____

_____

_____

_____

_____

_____

_____

_____

_____

_____

_____

_____

_____

_____

_____

_____

_____

_____

_____

_____

_____

Versandra Kennebrew

_____

_____

_____

_____

_____

_____

_____

_____

_____

_____

_____

_____

_____

_____

_____

Thank God for The Shelter: Memoirs of a Homeless Healer

Chapter Four

Forgive Yourself and Others

I lived with my father for maybe 6-months before we had the dreaded *"I think you need to move out"* conversation. I was furious. He said he couldn't deal with my younger brother, Thaddeus, who has moved with me and was just around 14 years old at the time.

You know how some boys are at that age. Their hygiene is not the best, and keeping things in order is almost impossible for them. It was not because I had not raised him right, either. He was just a dirty and disorganized boy. My father would say, *there is something wrong with that boy,* but I thought of him as my baby – and a mother's love protects; sometimes enables.

I admit that I'm not as much of a neat freak as my father, but I could definitely relate to not wanting to come home to see people and clutter in a house that used to have just one neat and tidy occupant. My father was taught well by the military to keep things in order. Wake up & *shit, shave and shower* was his routine. Because he was retired and didn't have much of a social life, the television kept him company.

My father was also the caregiver for my great-aunt Nook during that time. He would cook almost every day and take a plate to Aunt Nook at the nursing home. I didn't cook very often because my father didn't like my healthy style of cooking. He'd have a hissy fit if I cooked beans with smoked turkey or used the improper cooking utensil. I just let him do his thing in order to keep the peace. Besides all this, my father loved the attention he got from the ladies working at the nursing home.

For my own peace of mind, I retreated to my room when I was not working or at school. My waterfall and candles helped create an atmosphere of tranquility. I would primarily read my Bible and write in my journal. Television just seemed a waste of time to me.

The time Thaddeus and I spent at my father's house was difficult for everyone; new school, new city, new lifestyle. I would tell Tad that we were experiencing a temporary transition. Everyone was outside of their comfort zones and had to make the best of it until I finished school. I understood how this move may have affected him, because we had already moved from Alabama to Maryland. I felt bad about creating such an unstable environment. Here we were with my dad, where life was supposed to get easier. Tad had to enroll in another new school, which also meant testing and placement in another special education program. I had to be an understanding mom while also being a good daughter.

I tried to ease my father's trepidation by paying for biweekly house cleaning, but it was bigger than that. My father also thought I was crazy, especially after I shared with him what God was saying to me. My father told my family that, the next thing he knew, I would be selling bean pies on the corner. Don't get me wrong; I love my dad with all my heart, but I had to forgive him for abandoning me at a time when I really needed him.

I hadn't lived in Detroit since I was 12 years old. I didn't know anything about Detroit besides Southfield; the suburb where my dad lived. I'd been led to believe Detroit was violent and unsafe by the media. I was scared to drive past Eight Mile Road (the border where the city and the suburbs connected), and I was also confused as to why I got sick to my stomach each time I drove anywhere remotely near the east side of Detroit.

I didn't want to try getting a roommate and adjusting to different living styles again, so I moved into an apartment close to my dad. I found myself paying rent higher than my bud-get allowed, with no guaranteed salary, because I would soon be unemployed.

My father wanted the absolute best for his little girl. He had given me the experience of exploring Japan and Hawaii. He even wanted to rescue me from the stress of working 50-plus hours per week while raising my brothers alone. He wasn't prepared, though, for this rescue mission. Suddenly, a thirty-year part-time father was relinquishing his bachelorhood to his somewhat eccentric daughter and her brother, who was not even his son.

Sessions with one of my spiritual advisors revealed a childhood of trauma that had been suppressed. I had seen my mom after she had been gang-raped. I'd seen syringes lying all around my mom's house. I'd seen my sister and me climbing out of a window and down a tree to get out of the house, going in search of food to Grandma's house in the projects on the east side of Detroit.

After this *revelation*, I called my sister, Sheila, in Alabama, to verify everything. She did. Sheila remembered all of it, but I'd pushed the memories way down so that I could deal with my adult trauma. I may have coped by suppressing my childhood memories, but it was all coming back up, and my stomach was getting sick whenever I got close to where it all began.

I had to forgive myself for being so proud that I jumped out there, putting myself under more pressure than I could endure, instead of trying to work things out with my dad. Maybe I should have just moved back to Maryland. Every move I made from that point until the shelter was an act of survival.

Real logic has a hard time shining through desperation. More than that, my screwed-up mindset led me into another screwed-up marriage that I thought could change things.

Let me slow down a little bit...I have to mention that the entire time I was experiencing this transition, I was praying to God for peace and understanding. My sister Sheila and I would pray together long-distance over the phone. I embraced my prayer language during this time and I also learned the art of meditation. Thank God I did, because I would surely need these tools as I continued my journey.

I now know that if I had not forgiven my ex-husband, my father, my brothers, my mom and myself; self-hatred and discontent would have been like cancer, eating me alive. I could not have moved to my current place of unimaginable wealth if I had not released every care and every concern to God, who could recycle it and turn it into peace and love.

Affirmations

Repeat the following affirmations out loud three times each day for the next few days. See, feel and enjoy each experience as you say the affirmation.

Forgiving my parents allows me to be a better parent to my children.

Forgiving my former lover allows me to give and receive love like I have always desired.

I am forgiven. I am love.

Exercise 4

List five people who you believe have deeply hurt or betrayed you. It may have been a childhood bully, a family member or lover.

Now write those names on a piece of paper and place them in a wooden or metal bowl. Take your bowl of pain and disappointment outside to a safe open area and burn the contents. Step away from the flames, but stand there a few moments and feel the peace and love as it fills the space where anger and resentment once lived.

Use the space provided to write about how it feels to identify the source of your trauma and release it for good.

Journal

_____

_____

_____

_____

_____

_____

_____

_____

_____

_____

_____

_____

_____

_____

Versandra Kennebrew

_____

_____

_____

_____

_____

_____

_____

_____

_____

_____

_____

_____

_____

_____

Thank God for The Shelter: Memoirs of a Homeless Healer

_____

_____

_____

_____

_____

_____

_____

_____

_____

_____

_____

_____

_____

_____

Versandra Kennebrew

_____

_____

_____

_____

_____

_____

_____

_____

_____

_____

_____

_____

_____

_____

_____

_____

_____

Chapter Five

Be Open to Opportunities

Depression can be debilitating. Many days, I had to force myself to get out of bed. I had to resist the desire to drown my sorrows in alcohol and risky behavior. I chose to read, and one of the books I read was "The One-Minute Millionaire: The Enlightened Way to Wealth." It was two books in one. It shared information about creating wealth (which did not appeal to me at first), and it also told a story about a widowed mom who had to earn a million dollars to get her children back from their rich grandparents.

As I read her story, I saw myself in this mom's shoes and decided that I could do it, too. I could become an enlightened millionaire, and help not only my brothers, but also many others around the world.

After reading the book, I went to its website and printed out a certificate that marked the day I committed to becoming an enlightened millionaire. How could I dare say that I was going to get out of my financial and emotional mess and become rich? I had the nerve to even set a date – December 30, 2008. Frankly, I don't know how I dared to be so bold, but I did. It had to be the God in me who knew that I was a diamond in the rough, being refined through my shelter experience.

Reading *The One Minute Millionaire* was just the beginning of the library I would accumulate in my quest to become financially independent again. My first challenge was to get my massage business back on track. I began working harder, seeking more information and putting together a five-year business plan. I wanted to perfect the wellness resource center business model and open up centers all over Detroit.

There was no question in my mind about the industry I was supposed to be working in. Studies showed that complementary and alternative medicine was to be a trillion-dollar industry by 2012. People in general were not pleased with the traditional healthcare industry and wanted change. That year, Detroit had been named the fattest city in America, which meant that I was in the right location to make a difference. However, I had no money for marketing or advertising to let people know that I could help them.

My situation was like many other CAM professionals around Detroit, but the work I did to unite us to become more visible and help more people was not working. There had to be a way for us to pool our resources so that we could help more people.

I was in my office pondering this when a visitor walked in. He was a massage therapy instructor at a local massage school. He heard from an associate about the organization I was forming, and he wanted to learn more. We talked for a while, and he suggested that I come by the Dearborn campus and apply for a massage therapy instructor position that was available there.

When I got to the shelter that night, I couldn't wait to share the news. I told the other ladies about my potential job, and we were all encouraged by this ray of hope. Around that same time, one of my clients "gave" me a car. I gave him a few complimentary massages to show my gratitude, but you can't beat God's giving, no matter how hard you try. My new hoopty got me to the job interview with no problem.

My interview was with the director of education. We spoke at length about my experience as a massage therapist and as a former massage clinic supervisor and apprentice at another massage school. Those three years of experience were about to pay off. I had volunteered to assist the instructor with teaching massage, unpaid, for two years.

Our interview was interrupted by a fire drill, so we had to evacuate the building. I followed my interviewer, because I didn't want to leave that day without knowing I had a job. I had the chance to see most of the students I would be teaching, out there in the parking lot. I should have been more at ease during this break from the intense interview, which had brought me to tears several times, but my heart kept pounding because I was anxious and afraid.

I felt I needed to explain the emotions going on inside me, and my interviewer listened attentively.

She could see my passion for my work, and she thought my experiences would help me relate to some of the at-risk students there. My references were checked and I was hired that same week.

Teaching was cool. It was more demanding than what I had envisioned, but I loved sharing what I had learned about anatomy, physiology and pathology. I studied before classes like I was still in school to have a fresh perspective for my students. I learned to write lesson plans, make up quizzes, and teach students with various learning styles. Every day was a new adventure.

All the while I was gaining exposure for my business. I received the Spirit of Detroit award from the Detroit City Council in recognition of my leadership and commitment to enhance the quality of life of Detroit residents. I was also featured in the *Detroit News* and the *Michigan Chronicle*. I began writing articles about the healing power of touch. All was well with my new job, but I needed to really focus on my financial accountability.

I had to make sure I would never go back to where I was when I moved into the shelter. It was hard, because even though I was now making almost $20 per hour, I had to pay my accumulated debts. My time was running out at the shelter. This temporary place of refuge was going to soon be a memory, but I wasn't ready. I still needed to play catch-up with my bills.

It was hard to get an apartment because I had an outstanding balance at my previous residence. My COTS case worker was working with me, but the pressure was still on. A friend, Luis Gomez, who most people called *Angel*, came to my rescue and offered to share his home with me while I continued to get back on track. Angel was a massage therapist who worked with me as an independent contractor when I started my massage business in

Southfield a few years earlier. We kept in touch with each another after the post-September 11 economic slump made it difficult to keep open the doors of *The Healing Power of Touch Relaxation Center.*

Before September 11, we were on a roll. Our phones were ringing off the hook. My massage practice started with about 50 clients and grew to more than 500 clients, and six therapists.

I was not prepared at all for what September 11 would bring. As the twin towers were falling, so was my third marriage and my business. It was chaotic and I couldn't do a thing about it but try to hold on to my sanity.

I sold all of my beautiful office furniture for little or nothing, and another massage therapist and I moved into a shared office with a chiropractor. I put together a plan to pay off my debts, but that shared space problem reared its ugly head again.

It didn't work. The chiropractor was not happy with our arrangement. I was referring clients to him and thought we would make a great team.

When I moved in with Angel, it was to be for a few months. A few months turned into a couple years. All the while I was being healed. I will never forget how kind Angel was to me. We worked out a business arrangement that included a 2002 Grand Am for me. The books I was reading were teaching me the art of negotiation and so much more.

Some days Angel would sit in his easy chair, look over at me lying on the sofa and ask why I was crying? I would tell him I didn't want to be a burden on him, and he would tell me to take it easy and not work so hard. He assured me that I was in a safe place. He made it his business to massage my feet when I was stressed because he knew that foot massages helped relax my entire body.

He loved to cook on the grill and was an excellent host. I would often come home to stewed chicken or one of his other special Spanish dishes. Angel did the cooking and I took care of the rest of the house. We were a great team.

Angel, a mild-mannered, sexy, seasoned gentleman who once worked the farms of Puerto Rico, nurtured me. I was like an eagle with a broken wing. He took me home and mended me. He made sure I ate well and rested so that I would not get too overwhelmed; and like a loving father, when I was ready, he let me know it was time for me to fly – and that I did.

In December 2006, I moved into my own studio apartment downtown where I could see from my window the riverfront home I wanted. You see, while I was at Angel's house, I went to hear well-known motivational speaker Les Brown speak in a suburb of Detroit. Later I was his special guest at a weekend seminar that he hosted in Chicago. Les showed me how important it was to see those things that I desired in my mind and with my eyes.

I was however intrigued by Les long before our meeting in Southfield. In 1991, one of my customers lost all of his possessions in a fire, and Mr. Brown, who happened to be in the area, bought an entire wardrobe for him from the store I managed at the time.

A great mentor and motivator, Les Brown taught me that I could live my dreams. He taught me to stretch myself beyond my comfort level. Through his tapes, books and presentations, I learn to be accountable for my actions and choices.

I'm reminded of how I almost missed the opportunity to be mentored by him. When he invited me to Chicago, my first response was that I couldn't afford transportation. I guess I was expecting him to not only give me admission to an almost $2,000 event, but I wanted him to pay for me to get there.

My eyes were closed again to the possibilities. I could only see with my outer eyes. I didn't have much money, and bills were due, and any time off could cause me to lose even more money and so forth. I was having my own personal *pity party*.

Les told me that if he could provide the weekend experience that would change my life, surely I could find a way to get there. I got it. Fortunately, a good friend decided to drive me there, and we slept on the floor of her friend's apartment while we were in Chi-town. A sister's gotta do what a sister's gotta do! Oh, the people we met and the stories we shared…

All I can say is we, I, and you can do anything, everything, all things through the Christ consciousness within you. We can be our own worst enemies. Sometimes, we put these invisible obstacles in our own way. But I am a witness that there is no obstacle we can't overcome.

That motivational weekend in Chicago opened my eyes to the law of manifestation at work. T. Harv Eker says it like this: "Thoughts lead to feelings, feelings lead to action and action leads to results." Les, however, had our group of speakers and broadcast professionals to create "vision boards" with cut-outs from magazines that represented how we saw ourselves in three to five years.

I'm looking at my vision board now and it is amazing how it has expanded from about ten images to thirty. My vision board includes every- thing from healthy food to me and the man I love, embracing, looking out the window of my new riverfront condo. Some images have already been manifested, while others are on the way.

Let me break it down even further. Think for a moment, about one thing you and your family would do if money were no object. You could buy a new house with beautiful new furniture; a back yard with swings and a playground. You could take your family on a vacation. The sky's the limit.

Now, see you and your family enjoying a colorful, nutritious dinner in your new home. See yourself hugging and kissing your children goodnight. Feel the joy and excitement of knowing that all provisions have been met. Before you turn in for the evening, take a long soak in your hot tub. Close your eyes and breathe in the lavender and chamomile fragrance. Breathe in gratitude, breathe out loftiness. Breathe in love, breathe out fear.

I can't give you a timeline for when the results of your manifestation exercise will appear, but I'm sure you can see this process alone can give you peace in the midst of your storm. The feelings you get from visualizing yourself in your new home can last a lifetime. What an experience to be in the present and the future at the same time.

I am so thankful that I didn't miss that opportunity, because I am still friends with several of the people I met that weekend. We hold one another accountable for the goals we set. Our meeting that weekend was the beginning of a lifetime of friendship, personal development and mutual respect.

I can really say that after coming out of my temporary shelter, I was well equipped and ready to conquer the world. I had lost my mind so I could get a new one.

Affirmations

Volunteering my time and talents to support causes important to me are beneficial to me and the receiver of my gift.

My imagination is the preview of my life's coming attractions.

Opportunities are options for unity.

Exercise 5

The chart below will help you create a budget. Fill in the spaces of all that apply as accurately as possible. Add your totals from **B**, **C**, **D** and **E** together and place the sum in the total expense space at the bottom of the chart. Now bring the amount next to **A** down to the total income space. Finally, subtract your expenses from your income and place the difference in the appropriate space.

When your expenses are greater than your income, you have overextended yourself and need to make immediate reductions. If this is you, you have just identified yourself as being like millions of Americans, "one paycheck from being homeless." If this behavior has been evident for some time, seek *temporary shelter* immediately so that you can regroup and move on. For now, just acknowledge this fact by placing your initials in the space at the end of the chart. If you had prob-

78

lems being honest with yourself about the numbers or math required to complete the budget, acknowledge it and place your initials in the space provided.

*Move into a less expensive place of residence, have a garage sale to get rid of the excess and increase cash flow. Be a blessing to someone else while you control your controllables.

Income	
Wages	$
Interest/dividends	$
Miscellaneous	$
Income totals A	$
Expenses	
Home	
Mortgage/rent	$
Utilities	$
Home telephone	$

Cellular telephone	$
Home repairs	$
Home improvement	$
Home security	$
Garden supplies	$
Home totals **B**	$
Daily Living	
Groceries	$
Child care	$
Dry cleaning	$
Dining out	$
Housecleaning service	$
Dog walker	$
Daily living totals **C**	$
Transportation	
Gas/fuel	$
Insurance	$
Repairs	$
Car wash/detailing services	$

Parking	$
Public transportation	$
Transportation totals D	$
Entertainment	
Cable TV	$
Video/DVD rentals	$
Movies/plays	$
Concerts/clubs	$
Entertainment totals E	$
Total Income	$
Total Expenses	$
Difference	$
I am overextending myself financially and am at risk or homeless because of it.	Initial below _____
I have a problem with being honest about my finances and am at risk or homeless because of it.	Initial below _____
I have difficulty adding and subtracting the numbers to complete my budget and am at risk or homeless because of it.	Initial below _____

Use the following journaling space provided to write about your experience with creating win-win opportunities or the lack thereof. As you write, see yourself as the author of your life. Write to create or recreate. Do not beat yourself up if you feel inadequate in any area. You have the power to self-correct and re-write your own story.

Journal

_____

_____

_____

_____

_____

_____

_____

_____

_____

_____

_____

_____

_____

_____

_____

_____

_____

_____

_____

_____

_____

_____

_____

_____

_____

_____

_____

_____

_____

_____

_____

_____

_____

_____

_____

_____

_____

_____

_____

_____

_____

_____

_____

_____

_____

_____

Versandra Kennebrew

_____

_____

_____

_____

_____

_____

_____

_____

_____

_____

_____

_____

_____

_____

_____

_____

_____

_____

_____

_____

_____

_____

_____

_____

_____

_____

_____

_____

_____

Versandra Kennebrew

_____

_____

_____

_____

_____

_____

_____

_____

_____

_____

_____

_____

_____

Chapter Six

Watch Your Mouth

This place makes me sick...I'm broke...I'm tired...

I don't have any money...I can't do it...

They won't allow me...

Cancel, cancel with the power of love, is what my friend Carlista would say when these words came from my mouth. Before I was conscious of how I was speaking *death* and *lack* to myself, she knew the things we experience in our lives are manifestations of our words and thoughts.

Most people have heard of the Law of Attraction by now, but when I was in the shelter, I was not fully aware of its power. I let all kinds of crazy stuff come out of my mouth. Carlista would lovingly bring my awareness to what I was manifesting through my tongue.

Somehow, I was aware that being around people who were comfortable living in the shelter was not good for me. I also knew that having conversations with people whose greatest excitement came from getting a monthly check was a bad idea as well. So my best friend Carlista became my mainstay.

Carlista had to say *cancel, cancel with the power of love* a lot, so I guess I made a lot of statements that did not serve my highest good back then. I learned from experience that by saying, "that place makes me sick," I was manifesting just that; sickness. I thank God for Carlista, because her love and support lead me to the teachings from the book "Secrets of a Millionaire Mind." It was amazing. My church even did a weekly study of this book, which I recommend to anyone struggling with finances and other symptoms of negative programming.

"Speak those things that be not as though they were," is the scripture that comes to mind when I think about the power of the tongue. As I prepared to move into my new home, I remembered saying "my new riverfront condo is beautiful" or "I love my new home." I was saying this with no idea of when it would actually come to pass, but it felt good. I could actually see myself relaxing on my green chaise lounge, looking at the view of the river.

Think, see, speak, feel is my rule of thumb. My shelter experience taught me that, and T. Harv Eker put the icing on the cake when he wrote, "thoughts lead to feelings, feelings lead to actions and actions lead to results." You've done it before. You've thought about your favorite thing to eat. You've imagined yourself biting into it, tasting the delicious flavor and saying "I'm going to have _____ today."

As you enjoyed the feeling of that tasty morsel in your mouth, then going down your throat, the manifestation process had already begun. It may have taken a minute or even a month for you to get it, but if you take a moment, you will remember how good it tasted, and smile.

Just imagine using this same power to move you to the next phase of your life. Whether you are moving out of the shelter, out of your mom's basement or across the country, if you can think it, see it, speak it and feel it; it will be so.

But how can you change the negative thoughts and words that you have uttered most of your life? I'll be the first to tell you that it won't be easy. It may even hurt. I used the "rubber band method" as a pattern interrupter to pop myself when I spoke words that didn't serve me and immediately replaced them with words that did. In about thirty days, I felt cured, but kept another rubber band close by because negative thoughts would creep up at any time.

As I think about some of the things my words have manifested, it amazes me. For instance, when my brothers Tad and Isaac were growing up, I would tell them that I was working so hard for them so that they could live in clean, safe communities and go to great schools. I would always end the speech with the words; "I would be living in a one-room studio if I didn't have to take care of you guys." This is exactly what happened once my brothers were both grown and gone.

I would also say that when I left Angel's house, my apartment would be downtown and would have a river view. I wasn't very familiar with housing downtown before I moved there. I was familiar with the riverfront, where most of the city's festivals took place, and I knew downtown wasn't the ghost town that it was when I moved back to Detroit. I wasn't ready yet to purchase my riverfront home, but my words manifested me a little studio with a perfect view of the river and of my soon-to-be riverfront condo.

I guess I will tell you that I am currently manifesting the love of my life. He is passionate, loving and caring. He is eager to learn and experience new things including traveling with me around the world. He is brave and strong yet not controlling. He makes me laugh and gives a great massage. He is generous and never holds a grudge. He loves God and his family, and he demonstrates it not only through his provisions but through very frequent doses of loving touch. We share our thoughts and dreams and we love and support each other. We make great music together.

This manifestation thing is powerful. Just remember that you get what you say, write, think and feel, so be purposeful in your thoughts, words and deeds. I say I want to live in a clean, safe city so I don't stay inside complaining about dirt and crime. I walk around my city often, breathing in the fresh, clean air. I pick up debris sometimes and I engage people who look lost in conversations about peace and love.

Complaining is a big no-no, because it gives power to what you are complaining about. There really is good in every situation. It may take a little time to see it, but I promise it's there. Take, for instance, a dark and rainy day. The clouds are our protection from the hot sun, and rain provides water for humans and wildlife. It also equates to slowing down and enjoying an even more peaceful night's sleep. Dark rainy days are all good.

Affirmations

In this affirmation exercise, I would like you to bring the visual and audio together as you begin your "vision board." You will need to gather a few of your favorite magazines or other images of the life want to live in the future. Find images of your new home, your new business, the food you will eat to heal and support your body, the places you will visit, the money in your checking account, the money you will give to charity, your meditation and prayer space.

"Pinterest" and "Google Images" are also amazing options for an online vision board that you can take with you wherever you go.

Don't limit yourself to what you have seen in the lives of others. This is your chance to take your dreams out of your head and live them on paper or in the virtual world. You are manifesting your new life, so don't pass this opportunity up. No matter what anyone has said, you have the power to cancel it with the power of love and turn it into a life that is fulfilling and rich.

As you create your vision board, speak your vision into being.

I enjoy sitting on the rooftop patio of my condo by the lake.

My life and my home are organized and tidy.

My kitchen is equipped with cool gadgets and appliances and the colors and ambiance invite me to dance around preparing nourishing meals each day.

Exercise 6

I have listed a few negative phrases that I have heard today, and, in the column beside it, a positive substitute. Use the following spaces to practice doing the same. When this task is completed, get an empty jar and use it to drop a quarter in every time you make a negative statement. If you really want to change, you will be honest with yourself and drop the quarter in.

Each week, take the quarters and give them to a stranger with the message, "Your words have power." This is an exercise that will make you more aware and hopefully change your vocabulary; or you sow seeds into a stranger's life, helping them change as well. To reinforce the positive, you can deposit quarters in a separate jar to reward yourself when you abort a negative thought and choose to speak positively.

98

Negative	Positive
That's all right, I'm used to waiting	I'm sure I won't be waiting long.
Don't mind me. I'm nobody special.	You're excused.
No, I'm not beautiful. You must be kidding.	Thank you.
My spelling stinks.	
I don't speak well in public.	
I don't have the look you need.	
I'm broke.	
I hate where I live.	
I don't know how to do it.	

In the space provided, write about 3-5 situations that you at first believed were horrible and they turned out to be a blessing. How did you respond to or acknowledge your gift?

Journal

_____

_____

_____

_____

_____

_____

_____

_____

_____

_____

_____

_____

_____

_____

_____

_____

_____

_____

_____

_____

_____

_____

_____

_____

_____

_____

_____

_____

Versandra Kennebrew

_____

_____

_____

_____

_____

_____

_____

_____

_____

_____

_____

_____

_____

_____

Chapter Seven

Believe You Can

My friend Ifoma believes in me. We met at *4731 artist studios* when my wellness center was closed for renovations. What was supposed to be a temporary closure to put in a new ventilation system and build-outs turned into months of uncertainty, but again, I was not defeated. It was at *4731* where I embraced my inner artist and where my creativity was sparked again.

Ifoma, Funky Phil and some of the other artists adopted me as their sister. We spent a lot of time together in our *cluster of artists* studios. Sometimes we worked late, creating beautiful works of art. Painting, writing and building often called for music and snacks, which sometimes turned into an impromptu Detroit party. Funky Phil prepared his famous red cabbage slaw and gumbo, and we cooked out in the parking lot. We often came up with exciting events to showcase our work to the public. We encouraged and supported one another like family.

I told the artists about my shelter experience, but they didn't hold it against me. They let me tell my stories and allowed me to cry as I continued to be healed. I marveled at how my tears were no longer accompanied by anxiety. I cried tears of joy more often. I was gaining control of my life again.

Later, I learned why they didn't have much to say about my situation. I learned what the term "starving artists" really meant. I also learned that most artists were like massage therapists, in that they were highly talented and creative but they did not know how to manage their greatest commodity. They also didn't make enough money to hire someone else to manage it for them. I watched the *4731* artists create fabulous works of art, set up exhibits, and complain about the lack of customers just like massage therapists did. A change in perspective was needed.

So, I decided that I would help my new family learn everything I knew about business, so that their awesome work would be admired not only by me, but by the world. Helping others to be the best they can be has always given me much joy, but I had problems believing in myself sometimes. That is exactly why I loved *4731* so much. As I was giving, I was also receiving, and my new family loved me.

I began to share the motivational and personal development books I'd read. Audio books were easy to listen to while working, so they were our favorite. My *4731* family had no excuse for not hearing the words that inspired me as I danced through yet another crisis situation. I was getting stronger and stronger. Soon I would be ready to move into the next phase of my five year business plan. I had to wait for the renovations to be completed at *Northwest Activities Center* and my business to re-open. Then I would have cash flow and could invest in marketing the *Art of Touch DVD* I produced before my temporary business closure.

One day I read that one of the authors of "The One Minute Millionaire" was facilitating an *Enlightened Wealth* weekend retreat in Washington, D.C.. Ifoma and I had been infected by the books and had to get the experience live, so we decided to drive from Detroit to Washington, D.C. to attend the retreat.

Thousands of people came from around the world to be a part of this highly charged weekend of education and enlightenment. The facilitator, Mr. Robert Allen, was rich in so many ways. He

108

seemed to live what he taught in his book. He was the epitome of an enlightened millionaire, earning and giving while learning and mentoring.

I anticipated another dose of motivation like the one that prompted me to sign the certificate stating that I would be a millionaire by the end of 2008. I knew that I needed to be encouraged and motivated often while on my millionaire mission. Fear of failure popped up here and there, and I needed that positive energy to give me the strength to stomp on fear's ugly head.

Speaking of energy, that room of enlightened millionaire students was enough to cause an explosion. I'm sure the surge was felt all over Washington, D.C. and probably all the way back to Detroit. Enlightened wealth students received plaques and trophies for giving to charities, volunteering their time and talents and for reaching their financial goals. I was surprised, however, when I was given the invitation to come up to the stage to be acknowledged for demonstrating *courage in action.*

At first, I hesitated to get up because I felt that my accomplishment was less than the others, but it only took a few seconds for me to re-evaluate my thoughts and head to the stage. Ifoma and I travelled more than 900 miles to be present for this amazing event. I was worthy of applause from the several thousand people in the audience. So I made my way to the stage and accepted my trophy with great pride.

Smiling all the way back to my seat, I thought of all I endured over the last few years. I could never describe to Ifoma what I was feeling, so I tried to play off the excitement. After we left the retreat, we visited with my friend and artist, Wishum Gregory (aka Twitty), who lived in Maryland, just a few miles outside of Washington, D.C.

Twitty told Ifoma stories about the Versandra he knew ten years earlier. He talked about my strength and tenacity as I moved from the manager of one store to the market manager of 22 stores in three states. Twitty talked about my struggle to raise my brothers alone while pursuing my retail career. So many memories were ignited as we sat there talking about the good ol' days.

Seeing Twitty's Fine Art enterprise first-hand, and hearing the Les Brown story from the perspective of the house fire victim was also motivational for Ifoma. Twitty told us how he came to meet Les for the first time, and he shared colorful details about their relationship, which made me admire Les even more. You think you know a person and then you find out there is so much more to learn.

This trip helped me make the decision to close my massage studio and look for employment. I had come too far to begin falling. My marketing efforts were not getting new clients to my beautiful studio, and the hundreds of clients I had before closing, for one reason or the other, were not coming to visit me for massages. But, for the first time in a few years, I was feeling *healthy*. I was becoming an excellent money manager and my intuition was telling me to find employment that would teach me how to do business better.

I did not need a studio with additional expenses to achieve my next step, which was to get my credit repaired. What I needed was steady income until I was able to elevate to higher heights. I wanted to pay off a few debts and get prepared to move into my new riverfront home.

I not only believed I was ready to move on with my life, I believed I deserved to move on. In the following weeks, I would look for a job that would compensate me in more ways than one. I needed peace of mind, flexibility, and to interact with people. Being in an office would bore me to tears and I needed the energy of likeminded, creative people to feed me.

Exercise 7

In the space below on your left, list seven things that make you question whether you can achieve your goals or dreams. After compiling your list of perceived inadequacies, use the space on the right to list what you'll do to make the flaw disappear.

(example)	I am joining my local Toastmasters Club to improve my communication and leadership skills.
I don't communicate well	

Affirmations

Repeat the following affirmations out loud three times a day for the next few days. See, feel and enjoy each experience as you say the affirmation. In the spaces provided below, write three affirmations that reflect what you believe you can do with the power of God as your guide.

Health and wealth are my divine birthright.

I am attracting and inviting loving, supportive, beautiful relationships by loving myself in my entirety.

I am a positive role model and community leader.

I express love with my child by calmly teaching life lessons.

I love myself enough to set aside 30 minutes each day for self-care activities.

Journal

_____

_____

_____

_____

_____

_____

_____

_____

_____

_____

_____

_____

_____

_____

Versandra Kennebrew

_____

_____

_____

_____

_____

_____

_____

_____

_____

_____

_____

_____

_____

_____

Thank God for The Shelter: Memoirs of A Homeless Healer

Versandra Kennebrew

_____

_____

_____

_____

_____

_____

_____

_____

_____

_____

_____

_____

_____

_____

_____

_____

_____

_____

_____

_____

_____

_____

_____

_____

_____

_____

_____

_____

_____

_____

Chapter Eight

Surround Yourself with Love and Beauty

I had come to love how the arts stimulated my mind and emotions. I did not want to lose that feeling. As I tried to figure out my next move, I became anxious and was losing my mental clarity. I knew divine order would prevail, but at that time, I was still trying to be in control. Behind my smile was great trepidation.

Aromatherapy, yoga and meditation are all healing modalities that assisted me in getting back on my square. Plant essences like lemongrass and peppermint were both grounding and invigorating. Walking increased my circulation and stamina while allowing me to connect to nature and its natural beauty. And intentional, mindful breathing was a self-care ritual that often made distractions go "poof!"

As fate would have it, Kia, a supervisor at the Detroit Institute of Arts (DIA), came to an event I hosted at *4731*. Her energy was awesome, and the way she talked about the place where she worked sparked my interest. She met Ifoma earlier when she came by *4731* seeking donations for a silent auction for the DIA.

I did not want to be disappointed, so I avoided asking Kia about employment opportunities right away. Thinking back to elementary school, I could not remember visiting the museum. When she said it was one of the top art museums in the world, I was amazed. Why was this gem not a part of my childhood memories? Why was I not surrounding

myself with the energy and magnificence of artist-
ic creation?

The tall white columns, marble walls, waterfalls
and sculptures spoke architectural generous to my
soul. The grounds were always beautifully mani-
cured, and the most colorful people walked in and
out of this City of Detroit treasure. I wanted to see
what was inside this fabulous complex. Kia invited the artists of 4731 to be her guests for a Friday
Night Live performance at the DIA. There was
some resistance among my artist "family", but I
took it upon myself to persuade a few of the artists
to attend.

I was blown away. There was art everywhere. The
marble floors and the myriad of brilliant ceilings
captivated me. That particular night was Karaoke
Night, and Kia tried to talk me into singing in
front of all those strangers. The entire evening was

amazing, and I knew that the DIA was a place I would like to work, learn and grow.

Kia brought my attention to the African American art from the Walter O. Evans Collection. That experience was awesome as well. I have to admit that I knew little about fine art or art history when I first visited the DIA, but I was eager to learn. Besides, I wanted to become more cultured as I prepared to move to a new level of wealth.

For some reason, I thought wealthy people were cultured, but I came to learn that the opposite was true. Cultured people were wealthy, but not only with dollars and cents. People who enjoy art enjoy history. They enjoy freedom of expression. They enjoy life and living. Even homeless people came to the DIA to admire the art.

The stereotypes about people who don't have a home are ridiculous. Just like visitors to the museum were a mosaic of all types of people from diverse backgrounds converging into a collective consciousness, so are people who need shelter. Look around you. There are enough homes, money and food for everyone. The collective conscious-ness of people who are homeless appears to me to be that of lack and separation from *Source*. That certainly was the matrix I lived in then.

I finally got up enough nerves to ask Kia about jobs at the DIA. Somehow, all I could see was rejection, as she looked at me to see if I was seri-ous about my inquiry. Anxiety began to creep up on me again in the seconds that seemed like hours. As Kia contemplated whether to give me a refer-ral, my heart pounded. She smiled and suggested I stop by and complete an application, and my heart rate slowed down.

It was a long wait, but with Kia's recommenda-tion, in January 2007, I began working as a visitor service representative, assuring the guests of the

DIA had a pleasant and unique experience. I had to learn the layout and programming for the museum. Everything was new and exciting. I was able to meet people of every culture and race as if I were back in Maryland. I now got paid to express my gratitude for meeting cool people and showing them around one of the most beautiful places in the world.

Love and beauty raises our vibration. When we vibrate higher, we manifest the desires of our hearts. Blessings flow! Or, as Rev. Ike would say; "the feeling gets the blessing." If you want to graduate from where you are, you must change your vibration - adjust your frequency so that a different energy and different results will be drawn to you.

Moving into the *4731* studios and then getting a job at the DIA were only a couple of examples of how the principle of surrounding myself with love and beauty assisted me in transitioning from my shelter vibration to one of abundance. There were many other examples. To this very day, I am moved by experiences I envision as lovely and beautiful in my mind.

My favorite example of this principle takes place in a recurring vision where I dance my prayers to God in my secret garden. The flowers and trees also sway in their sacrifice of praise to the Creator, and there is nothing but love.

The point I want to leave you with is that we create our own realities. In the midst of pushing our way through life transitions, we are creating a new world of our own choice and of our own design. Ask yourself; what do I want my new world to be like? Who do I want to serve in my new world? How do I want to feel in my new world? Who will be with me in my new world?

I'm not talking about getting in a spacecraft and traveling to another planet. I'm simply saying that what you see on the news does not have to be your reality. Despair, depression and financial chaos do not have to dominate your life just because you have become comfortable with it. You are the only one who can choose what your reality will look like. Once you choose, you will need to make moves toward the reality you desire and then buckle up for the ride.

After a few months working at the DIA, I learned that the museum would also be closing for renovations. This time, I did not see closing as a negative; I chose to see it as an opportunity. I chose to see this temporary closing as a period of reflection, and that it was.

The guests were gone, but the museum was committed to keeping their employees working during the closure. Many of my days at work turned into hours securing low-traffic areas in the museum, which allowed me to research and write. God was giving me the opportunity to write the vision and make it plain. So while others were complaining about being bored and not having anything to do, I was thanking God for the job and the opportunity to fine-tune my business strategy while getting paid.

Have you ever seen a person who was not in school, but they seemed to walk around with a pen and paper all the time? Think about it for a moment. You probably thought they were crazy when they appeared to move from an entranced state, to frantically writing like their life depended on it. If you haven't seen it before, pay closer attention, and watch how what I call "brain storms" are showering people all over the world. People are becoming more and more in tune with their divine purpose.

Once your eyes have been opened to your purpose in life and the infinite possibilities, your thoughts expand, and so do you. Some people think they are losing their mind, but they are actually finding it. That notebook of brain storms is probably the blueprint to another million-dollar idea or invention, or a plan to heal the world while amassing a fortune. Maybe it's a map to your new home.

In addition to the creative ideas that were flowing through me, I was also learning how to prepare for a grand reopening. And grand it was. The excitement of the new DIA made me think of the celebration I would have when I manifested my first million dollars, so in preparation for that special day, I hired a limo to take me and one of my millionaire friends to a beautiful restaurant to dine. That night we encouraged one another to continue setting goals and work the plan that God had given each of us.

In this memoir, I have proposed the following to help you conquer homelessness or any other major life transition: Find a Place of Refuge, Count Your Blessings, Look in the Mirror, Forgive Yourself and Others, Be Open to Opportunities, Watch Your Mouth, Believe You Can, Surround Yourself with Love and Beauty. These principles helped me stay grounded and healed me as I blossomed into a woman of great wisdom and great wealth.

So, do you want to know if I manifested the river-front condo I spoke of throughout this book? Do you want to know what I wrote in those note-books while working at the DIA during renovations? Maybe you are asking yourself; how can this book transform my life right now?

Well, let me tell you like this. I not only have everything I need; I am whatever I believe. I manifest my heart's desire always. And so do you. Go back and read this book again and don't forget the exercises this time if you did not get a major breakthrough.

Delano Willis, a gentleman I met at Café DIA one day, read my story and said to me, *"It looks like you want a condo on the river."* I conferred and we discussed his riverfront condo which would be available in April 2009. When the engine in my car went out and $1500 was needed to repair it, I focused on my dream. When my credit was still in repair and my savings account couldn't handle the burden, I affirmed, *"I am wealth beyond measure."*

I had to go in deep with my daily manifestation regimen if I really wanted to move into my new home by December 2008. Not only did my angel, Sasha, appear, brining me a new Dodge Caravan to drive for free while I continued my book signing schedule, I also received a call from Delano, the homeowner, informing me that December would in fact work out if I could pull together $15,000. A poverty mentality will not allow you to believe in miracles.

I showed up to take a tour of Delano's condo even though my bank told me I could not get a home loan for $15,000. I showed up to meet with Delano and his attorney to discuss the purchase of my condo even though I had less than $100 in the bank. I believed I would move into my condo before the end of that year, even though I had less than 90-days to raise the money for the purchase of my new home.

Even on the closing date, miracles were still being manifested as angel Kimle appeared to loan me the final $2000 I needed to purchase my home. She said God told her to help me reach my goal. December 27, 2008 I went to closing with a $6,000 cashier's check. Delano sold me his condo for the amount that was to initially be my down payment. He told me about his own homeless experience

132

before he became a psychologist. I cried tears of joy as I signed the deed to my new home.

That same day, I moved into Shoreline East Condominiums, a beautiful gated community with a doorman and a rooftop penthouse on the Detroit River. The red carpet was rolled out. As you can see, divine order prevails.

My name is Versandra Kennebrew and I am a homeless success story. My greatest desire and life's purpose is to remind humanity of its divinity. I asked God who I was, and this is the answer I received.

"I am the quintessence of the divine, most perfect of all creation. With power to produce at will, seeds that multiply like ripples in an ocean. The personification of I AM, beautified, radiating, absolute and undeniable. I AM Love."

Affirmation:

I love myself enough to study, practice and deliver excellence.

I add value to the lives of everyone I come in contact with.

I surround myself with people who love and support me.

Exercise 8

Place your right hand on your left shoulder and your left hand on your right shoulder. Now squeeze. Self-care is the manifestation of self-love.

In the following space provided, write about the most beautiful experiences you've ever had. If nothing comes to mind, take a moment and dream about experiences you would like to have, then write about them.

Journal

_____

_____

_____

_____

_____

_____

_____

_____

_____

_____

_____

_____

_____

_____

_____

_____

_____

_____

_____

_____

_____

_____

_____

_____

_____

_____

_____

_____

Thank God for The Shelter: Memoirs of A Homeless Healer

_____

_____

_____

_____

_____

_____

_____

_____

_____

_____

_____

_____

_____

_____

_____

_____

_____

_____

_____

_____

_____

_____

_____

_____

_____

_____

_____

_____

_____

_____

_____

_____

_____

_____

_____

_____

_____

_____

_____

_____

_____

_____

_____

_____

_____

_____

_____

_____

_____

_____

_____

_____

_____

_____

_____

_____

_____

_____

_____

_____

_____

_____

_____

About the Author

Versandra Jewel Kennebrew is a metaphysician, Master Touch Artist and Certified Holistic Health Coach. She has made a wealth of contributions to those seeking health and well-being through her global wellness ministry.

An international speaker, she has wowed audiences large and small from Montreal Quebec to Bali Indonesia. Her nearly 20-years of experience in the healing arts allow her to fuse personal development with holistic health to empower and transform lives.

Kennebrew enjoys training marriage ministry leaders, counselors and healing artist to become Certified Touch Artists. Through this intimacy and relationship enhancing program, she is touching the world literally.

The author of four self-help books and contributor to several anthologies or multi-author publications, Kennebrew values being a competent communicator and continuing education. Versandra Kennebrew is a proud member of Toastmasters International and executive leader of her club in Atlanta, GA. To request Ms. Kennebrew as a speaker for your upcoming wellness or relationship enrichment conference, expo or retreat, visit:

www.VersandraKennebrewIntl.com.

OTHER PUBLICATIONS BY
VERSANDRA KENNEBREW

Made in the USA
Middletown, DE
20 November 2016